# The Empathy of Rain
## A Collection of Poems

Verde Mar

NFB Publishing
119 Dorchester Road
Buffalo, New York 14213
For more information visit Nfbpublishing.com

Dedication

For Calliope, et tu.

A deeply heartfelt thank you to all the incredible writers in the online global social media writing community who have supported my writing since I began writing poetry at the start of the global pandemic.

Dedicated with love to my mother, Florence, and to the loving memory of my mentor, Dr. Linda Buzzeo Best.

# ALSO BY VERDE MAR

*The Empathy of Rain*

*Entangled Universes Trilogy*:

Book 1: *Turbulent Waves: Enigmatic micro-writes cast ashore during a global pandemic*

Book 2: *A Wave Without a Shore: Enigmatic poetry cast across the universe*

Book 3: *Tides of Light* (forthcoming)

Contributing author:
*Hidden in Childhood: A Poetry Anthology*

Edited by Gabriela Marie Milton; published by Literary Revelations

Night finds us sharing a time when only poets and lovers
know how to find their way to dawn; all of us are both.

If poets decide the menu our hearts choose from, our
lovers and friends write the recipes we cook from
throughout our short lives in this entangled universe.

# Contents

# PROLOGUE

Rain has a deep emotional connection to our conscious and unconscious minds. Psychologically, the sounds of rain are soothing and provide us with a sense of calmness. Rain even has an evolutionary aspect in humans since we are essentially social animals and our ancestors spent lots of time outside in nature. In addition, rain also has a physical connection to us: air pressure and relative humidity changes can affect our mood and stress levels.

The subtle smell of rain can also remind us of peace and rejuvenation. One example is the effect of petrichor, the pleasant smell that frequently follows the first rain after a period of dry weather. The human sense of smell is sensitive to geosmin, a chemical compound with a musty, earthy odor. Some researchers believe that humans appreciate the rain scent because our ancestors most likely relied on rainy weather for their survival.

The idea of empathetic rain also extends beyond these physical and psychological effects to the point where it plays a part in how a writer or a poet draws energy from such effects, including the various sounds of rain, in the act of creation. This anthology includes the poetry I have written listening to the diverse types of sounds in nature, and in particular, music compositions.

Writing poetry is like meeting someone you've known forever for the first time; you have no idea that you will be entangled throughout many universes, but the vibe never fades away each time you dance in the arms of your muse. Her language embraces us, yet the semantical dance begins as if we have never met, so the poet is left wondering when we part how much of our song stays with you as the lingering poetic resonance walks you home?

The anticipation of a new write begs that we forget about everything else as the beat, the flow, and the cadence of her dance grips your mind after you release the first few words; it's as if the remaining lines have been waiting for us to catch up with them as they casually cascade out of our minds.

Eventually all of us will share thoughts in some form of poetic meter. It's almost as if language and thought conspire to find a common ground or alkahest, where we all playfully trade linguistic charades as all of us learn to wield our thoughts into something we have yet to imagine. Thinking in poetic verse changes our meter of thought. It's as if we capture a wider state of understanding within a smaller linguistic context. Like a song's melody might uncover a deeper empathy, poetic meter measures the separation of sound and meaning; it's like a dance we never stop learning.

The poetic mélange releases us to search for the song of ourselves; Calliope never wavers to fly with you if you're willing to soar in unknown skies without fearing how others interpret where your sojourn might take us. Stories are hidden everywhere in plain sight. Touch a surface and its history pleads for you to be one with it. In dark days when society is unstable and unsure of who we are becoming, be true to yourself and share the poetry only you have the power to unveil. It is rain's transformative nature that provides our imagination with the leap of faith to believe that what was once inside us, gathers strength to enable us to spread our wings.

In the night, poets race to unmask the silence of an unborn poem. Her life so fleeting, it's as if our language cries to embrace what might have been before her wings take flight against the vast darkness of the forgotten. When you write something that brings chills or captures your imagination in a way nothing else has garnered such a thought within you, the act of writing a poem becomes much more than the meaning of the words themselves.

Poetry shows us that everything we experience means something completely different to a person you've known and loved your entire life, almost as if a thousand universes surround all of us every day and each decision we make, each interpretation of a song, an emotion, a word rewrites that poem, feeling, music, or choice so that when we finish it our tears still come from the same one we all share.

Light is poetry unbound; we ourselves are instantiated poems birthed by the sun. Light is not defined by one color; everyone you see is part of you. If I write a poem thinking of yours know that such shared light has always been together in one form or another shared between us. Our eyes never see the real you; everyone gathers mirrored and reflected light to construct images that approximate your truth.

# MORNING DEW

*But words are things, and a small drop of ink, falling like dew, upon a thought, produces that which makes thousands, perhaps millions, think.*
*- Lord Byron*

## Empathy's Rain

*She loves empathy's rain*
*Like a star's first light blossoms in the vast night*
*Entangled thoughts rush out to find their words*
*To be reborn again in our silent quantum space*
*Forever wings lift us with our luminous souls.*

# Becoming a Poet

There were times I wondered where to start
Like tonight as my mind unfolds your memories
A maze of emotional gates unleash them now
They recapture thoughts I've let go free since.

All of the sharp turns a heart makes just to feel
When the road is silent our bodies wait to play
You sing of what it means to become a poet
I write of what it means to read love into yours.

Time has her way with musings I've employed
Sharing them seems a plea for deeper secrets
I wonder of my short years writing as a new poet
What will I find as I work my way home to you?

## Dreams of You


In between dreams your breath bakes what's left
We move as if there's only one to find what's real
By dawn you remember what we both shared
I write love letters to the ghosts of who we were.

You hold me to my promise as no one understands
Even our music tries to capture what's left of us
How does it feel to read my words as yours leave
Moments ask if it's too late to bridge love and time.

Days have become mirrors of our lost thoughts
Our rain asks if it's time to let them go into forever
We've always known when our pages turn away
I'll dream of you again someday when we're ready.

# The Poem in Your Eyes

In the end of days our ancient memories persist
We've grown old replaying them under such skies
Stories tell of how we grew into these new shells
Under lost light of these realizations I hold yours.

A poet consumes time like a storm serves her rain
Each of us writes to music that finds our Calliope
There are nights when such memories dream me
When you are alone do they touch you as well?

Time cascades like painted charms in new words
Their wonder persists like our very first smiles
Windows of happenchance unveil treasures left
The look you gift to me becomes another poem.

# Wondrous Stories in Your Light


There was a time we shared our poetry like rain
Each moment umbrella'ed our wings as we soared
My eyes became mirrors as your light took me
Out of the maddening noise just to share a smile.

I've known deep souls here who play my songs
Others whatever it takes for me to learn why not
A poet writes as a muse opens our minds to you
When you hear your melody it's your soul in mine.

I've read wondrous stories within your embrace
Almost as if we've entangled ourselves in forever
Still, as light of this one ebbs know that I love you
Our rain will always be poetry no one else writes.

# Time Plays Us Straight

After our play ends today asks if now's the time
Your eyes full of songs even Dylan has yet to pen
Laughter meets a complete unknown in mine
Relief saunters as if we've just decided our fates.

My empty wine glass cries for your piano player
We share tales of a kiss under a crescent moon
It's alright now as our future has lost us in thought
No one ever mentioned that time plays us straight.

We're no longer who we were that moonlit night
You sing of a time we wrote our lost poetic plays
I measure time that no longer knows how to begin
In an evening of sanity even a poet needs a home.

# The Rapture of an Intuitive Storm


Empathetic rain saunters like your sad eyes know
We've played under her skies like ghostly lovers
Days when only tears could find storms we owned
As if their magic always knew our tide would turn.

Its touch a rare moment as a shy sun reappears
When we walk a path unbidden of rules, we're free
In a time when love's effortless joy danced with us
You were always the rain I needed to feel inside me.

If our eyes windowpane what emotions can become
I've always felt yours like a thunderstorm enraptures
Hearts so deep-felt as we collect our intuitive sighs
Find me again on a day the rain asks if we're ready.

# Rainstorms that Touch Our Yesterdays


Rain pianos us like breath sings of our desire
Across a night's lingering light yours finds mine
Such petrichor entangles a poet's language
As if your scent has become mine overnight.

Her gentle touch plays as yesterday asks to stay
Heartbeats save moments like a glance loves
I write imaginary ballads in empathetic storms
Your mind, my anchor as everything else leaves.

Our aftermath komorebi's light in starved eyes
Like morning dew all over pages we've written
We read our new light as if it's a newborn story
As I hold onto your parting glance, love crushes.

# The Poetry of Becoming Us

A lost sky violins her rain all over our masks
Like a moment you realize no one is waiting
Thoughts of you flower even as I walk alone
Words trade secrets like a meme steals ours.

We met on a page even time can never leave
Where have you taken me as you disappear
Calliope holds my heart and soul in this light
As it ebbs & flows I wonder if you'll remember.

There's a reason love's flame never dies here
Surrounded by darkness no one comprehends
Our music & poetry streetlight the way we are.
On a road no one shares yours makes up mine.

# Of Days No One Knew Who We Were

Surrounded by uncertainty's unwritten premise
Even daring streetlights unveil false prophets
When a poet shares her silence, listen to her
Debates we dine on tonight have no recourse.

The space of being us asks if you're ever ready
A question we all need to answer just once
I'm thinking about who we were all those days
I'd read Rimbaud and Dylan to you all night.

A kind of beautiful light wandered across us
We danced umbrella'ed under taken promises
Kindness our only garden played us all night
So we rolled today's forever dice just to be sure.

# Light Under a Faded Moon

If only I could recall our words that found us
Jewels of approximation that asked for our eyes
On a wave that carries us across this universe
Each pause wonders if it's time to look around.

Your magic casts our image like a mirrored lens
My light burns for you as a dying candle pleads
One step closer and our sun asks if we're real
As if who we are stops to pray for who we were.

I tried to tell you as empty thoughts blossomed
You are the river asking our light for forgiveness
Under a lonely crescent moon I wrote about you
My lost words hold on tight as you've faded away.

# The Lost Languages of Love

You told me nothing changes as the sun fades
Seeds of this lie garden the first look you made
Reality settles all over our final nonchalance
I remember who we were as truth dined on us.

Landscapes blanket surreal languages within us
Their measure becomes what we use to be love
Left alone words wander within us still hopeful
I have read yours over lands and many lifetimes.

So we still walk under this golden sun amused
Steps footprint both of us as we find our paths
A new sunrise wonders if light still makes us up
Both of us umbrella it as we decide what's real.

# Echoes of Our Song in a Poem

In another time, our children's eyes sang sadly to ours
Bereft cobblestone streets walked home in time with us
Our naked feet laughed racing between their icy curbs
As a full moon blushed whispering incognito love songs.

You tempt me under a new sun today as if they were us
Music we recall writes of poetry that imagines them
Event horizon storms masquerade like our first kiss
Tomorrow saunters into us like an unfound memory.

A woman looks to us as we realize she is our yesterday
All we know rewinds as I look through a stranger's eyes
You catch your breath as her poetry paints who we are
I wrap my words in yours as we surrender to her rain.

# The Study Of Us

As a prophecy danced with our tears we knew
Stars fell the night when we lost a forever poet
The kindness of time plays us like lost lovers
Mirrored glances find what hearts save for last.

If to fall is to study the teacher and the student
How far will a patient mind walk with us here
The empathy of an unknown soul who knows
As what light decides to share holds our breath.

We play within ancient tales that ask us to stay
Is it because what is to come will unmake us?
A child of the sun doesn't remember the heat
Yet as a fire of love dissolves us, I'll wait for you.

# The Sound of You

A poet stops to listen when everyone leaves
We're just looking to share words in silence
When yours gives up on mine is anything left?
We read what's still real when we're all alone.

Wampanoag paths still call my riparian youth
Riversides rushed to sketch a love against truth
Broken minds sought higher ground as we left
In the mirror of your eyes my poetry says hello.

Friendship wanders in a lonely night with Love
They frolic just to share a song under the moon
When you're lost in a silent night alone, sweet
Listen to the sound of your gentle mind talking.

# Inside Her Eyes, Outside Time

Deep prophecy cast within her lithophanic eyes
I saw myself years from now under a strange sun
She walked beside me as red sunlight painted us
Her lyrical voice mesmerized mine into silence.

Unstuck between both worlds terror stalked me
Never fear love, she whispered returning in time
Mountains cloaked in blue mist rose ahead of us
A lucid sigh shrouded thought and she was gone.

Years have passed since time flooded that day
Her vision returns when our yellow sun reddens
As if I could sense her piercing glance all over me
Was it just a dream I had such a long time ago?

# Fading Realizations

Water wonders why our eyes are so dry here
Pools of our thought run together in our rain
My mind stripped blind of your precious light
Everything I've lost without you prays for us.

You make morning seem like she's been here
Sipping on light both of us left in her lost rain
My reach wonders do you want me dear one?
Words mob flash with your friends as you fade.

My shore so alive in our footprint shadows now
It's as if your poetry writes us here as ghosts
They crowd in my mind like friends who debate
I'm left alone sipping on our lost thoughts.

# Dream Box

She journeys alone in a box of your dreams
It's four in the morning and you're gone
Lying on a bed each of them touch the sky of night
On a shore only forever's patience awaits.

All these moments I have lived through many times
They cradle my thoughts like your smile
Yet, everyone slowly disappears like the rain
Until another sun appears and we begin again.

# VIRGA

*Virga are trails of precipitation that fall from the underside of a cloud but evaporate or sublime before they can reach the earth's surface.*

## Our Forever Waltz

*Silhouettes komorebi all along our pasts*
*As time's amber gently releases them*
*Yet the urge to hold on whispers to us*
*All along those moments we've shared.*

*I still feel the light from within your eyes*
*Come will you and walk with me there*
*One more time to find our forever waltz*
*As the sky has become a poem of you.*

# The True and the Real


First words rave into our minds on a rouge wave
It's as if they're our children rushing ahead of us
Playfully opening secrets buried away lost in time
Each one asks why have we been away so long?

Still a day is long as they fill us up with meanings
It's as if when we dance they hide behind a smile
Like everything we save just to make them real
I've been here all day thinking what you might say.

By now the rain has forgotten to cloud my desert
Yet I can still taste what you meant in sweet words
Waves of compassion ask if what we say is true
When a poem is born she gives birth to our light.

**Poetry Rains Like Forgotten Moments**

Wonder, a child's prism never lets us go
she walks us home even in our darkness
her magic introduced us when we first met
Love, her rogue sister winks as we begin.

We start over as our poetry rains inside us
rainbows on the day of our execution plead
blue streetlights cry for us in lost chances
your eyes write who you are all over me.

Our moments slip into a cup we never drink
a new song plays what love meant to us
her dance moves against us like a lover
our shared glances anchor the night.

# Thought as a Jewel Only Our Fire Can Sustain

You feel my glance like a touch asks for another
Wonder sits outside alone as we decide her fate
As I comply, our breath simultaneously becomes
A sudden shift in our sighs bridges us back to her.

Together again almost as if light is hysterical now
We measure a distance in between our thoughts
They dance behind our eyes like hidden jewels
Each one sparkles in a fire only we might sustain.

I feel yours like an angel's wings settling within me
Every time I think of you, astonishment says hello
All these words have always been yours as I write
Drink them with me as seduction's mood plays us.

# Light's Surrealistic Umbrellas

We step into broken light's maddening shadows
Doppelgänger thoughts sip on our morning's dew
They consume ours under surrealistic umbrellas
We all share reality in a moonlit komorebi dance.

Sunrise's wanderlust beckons what's found now
It's as if newborn light delights touching our eyes
I share my look as your glance lingers in a poem
Your words written inside me embrace both of us.

Images hidden behind our mirrors ask to be freed
It's as if we've always known what new light unveils
When your hand touches mine such thoughts stay
My eyes full of what yours share, rain love again.

# Desire's Archipelago

Keepers of the red glow candle our minds
Sol says goodnight with fire on our horizon
You garden mine throughout the dark night
Dawn joins our ménage à trois in light's kiss.

A panting lover's quest asks you for another
Rain's sudden serenade mixes our mimosas
Desire's archipelago unmasks lonely shores
Even the grateful dead still play music for us.

A vibrant sky wanders past as thought agrees
I write of twilight darkness behind your eyes
It flowers as my words paint you in the light
Lost love escapes just as we leave in smiles.

# Keeping Up with Our Words

Yours is a touch that sustains our place in time
Hers is the look that devours our imagination
Ours is a space we make just to find ourselves
I was the mirror you always forget in the night.

We're not who we were and there's no way back
So you simmer my last glance like you know me
In between such moments our lust gasps for air
It's just a matter of time before we surface again.

Poetry asks if we can keep up with these words
I sleep on everything you've ever shared with me
Each time I read you, you become someone new
Mine is a touch that wonders if you're still real.

# Planting Seeds of Future Poems

You touched me down in my bones that rainy day
Seeming like a storm in a word our eyes flowered
Most of the time when I think of you I'm all alone
Even dark skies can't end such moments with you.

A sigh plays melancholic piano like Bill Evans could
Harvesting seeds we planted when we first met
It's a song no one else has ever shared, sweet
It wasn't what we expected, as the rain fell on us.

We're still the same wide-eyed souls who love this
On a moonlit shore our footprints follow laughter
Treasures that wait for a wave that finally found us.
Each one of them lapping against what we made.

# Melancholy's Ghost

January's angel touched me with an afternoon kiss
As she spied Melancholy's ghosts dining on my mind
Like lost desert rain that never finds the ground here
She weeps as they huddle together waiting in the sky.

We met one day as a lover's glance bid me farewell
You will learn to sleep with me as my dreams are yours
And as the days fall in love with years, I will never leave
Let me fill the rooms of your mind with my children.

Her eyes implored, why do you love everyone, darling?
Desert sand covered a blue sky as lips prayed to answer
Yet only the sun could taste my desolate reply to her
Like the rain, my words stolen away by her sweet breath.

## Mischievous Intentions

What did you see in my eyes as a cold rain fell
Electricity stretches as time changes our games
Frozen glimpses decide our fate as seconds tick
Worlds fall away between us as we make ours up.

All your thoughts run through mine in this light
I write to a lover, Melancholy in case you leave
She asks my friend Calliope to join our new dance
Bold moments of being us strike like lightning.

Your vibrant touch opens doors of my perception
I can sense your heat as you decide on mine
Fire finds another surface as your smile debates
We lubricate what remains with mischievous intentions.

# Lost Goddesses

Sometimes your silence becomes my brazen sky
Our remaining words just lost clouds raining away
We've lost spaces between them like time fades
Silent star's gaze reigns as they take your place.

They tell me Love is a lost goddess looking for us
On a night when even hundred-dollar heat chills
I can hear what you're thinking but no one's here
Melancholy has asked me out on a date, dear lover.

I remember that day you discovered a lost poet
We talked as years had forgotten what time meant
Dylan wrote electricity's ghost howled in our faces
As if he knew what became of the days we shared.

# Vintage Treasures


As the sky rose by dawn I knew you loved another
Light can be a lover or a taste that sears a heart
In between your images imagination loses sleep
How does love left behind climb out of my bed?

Our high tide laments the sea without us anymore
Oceans of thought change minds as we hold on
We keep treasures only you and I recognize now
Each new day fades as if it never happened to us.

Hold on asks each new sky just to color our hope
Yet time isn't a vintage we've never tasted before
In the wild woods where hearts all sleep together
I will look for yours one last time before I leave.

# Enticement of a Poetic Glance

A lonely soul catches fire as your words ignite her
She cooks them with light within and smiles back
Astonished as hers were just playing in your mind
Between all our words enticement glues us together.

Her sigh sings of your name as if you were a poem
Stray heat slips between each line she wrote back
Lost thoughts meander as if we both know our way
She writes one for you that strikes her fire within you.

We met listening to Dylan's masterpiece in the dusk
Your laughter asks if I know what you mean now
His lyrics line the corridors of our minds
Just as mine becomes a firestorm inside your eyes.

# Rainstorm Train Stations

You waited as our rain became empathetic notes
Windowpanes play melodies no language speaks
You're the breath on a frozen night that holds me
Vehicles of passion crisscross our silent glances.

We hold time as bubbles in rain saving butterflies
Each thought wanders alone until we gift it wings
When yours comes home in the dark embrace her
All our moments sandcastle what we know is true.

My silhouette plays games all over your surprise
It's as if our poetry makes us up over in each line
A midnight train waits for us to decide if it's true
When you buy your ticket will you sit next to me?

# All These Words…

Eyes write of shared love like poetry reminds us
I found a mirror inside your soul looking out at me
A moment suddenly all alone lights a lonely fire
We both learn to play the piano left between us.

When the rain leaves us still wanting to feel more
There's only you left for me to hold on to now
As my light ebbs and your sunrise begins to shine
All these words fall like starlight waiting for yours.

Never caged, love's metaphor makes you up here
Sudden butterflies decide our fate as we fly away
Our poetry borrows gifts you leave inside my heart
As we both soar in new skies our song takes us.

# Our Bridge of Light

Should we fall out of these skies in our winter
Chasing what was and what might have been
Woven between our eyes a bridge of light sings
Threads we weave in glances that never let go.

Our tides forever cross these oceans of night
Time becomes the amber our dance slips inside
Your look frees the souls of our unspoken words
For me, the moment wanders as we touch a find.

Yours is the real, mine is the truth that entangles
All these moments have become the rain inside
My wings unfolded settle around you in darkness
Creatures of light we weave our thoughts together.

# Playing In Our High Tides

It's not just about our skyline's temperaments
Your jazz and conversation always rain inside me
When we walk under her full moon eyes dance
Even shy stars wink as we find another high tide.

A gaucho moment shares a glimpse of who I am
You wonder as our storm turns into a saxophone
Glitterati ghosts play us under amber streetlights
Night maidens sing charms as supple eye candy.

In time with racing visions in tangible electricity
Our sustained poetic sighs walk both of us home
My touch asks questions both of us are thinking
Waves have us now as we both dive under again.

# The Lonely Rain Inside Our Forever Dance


In the winter of souls love anchors our desire
Tides of emotional resonance lap new shores
Your look carries past lives as if we've been reborn
Only strange winds know what we harbor by now.

All of my words wander like a dream no one's had
Your poetry spans landscapes only dreamers see
A song of us falls like lonely rain wanting to dance
Wings settle just as we both decide to stop time.

Entangled inside what's true and real laugher spills
Only mirrors capture us as no one can see our real
Ghosts of our entwined music play inside our eyes
Their desire seeps out as each of us takes flight.

# Planting Flowers in Our Box of Rain


Dusk drapes her asteraceaes high above our box of rain
An intimate deep blue moon dances with lonely songs
As a touch of sapphire glitters inside your gorgeous eyes
I'm caught in your slipstream as their light captures mine.

We write our lives like dying flowers in love with the sun
Such short time we blossom here yet love never ends
A stranger tastes your gorgeous as she devours our real
My words grow seeds of thought reminding me of yours.

You've found me in the mirrored light we've become
Such imagined visions as you rewrite us with one look
Eyes that open perception's door as I walk through it
Such is the light we hold as true when we read yours.

## Tempting Visions of Your Poetic Elixir

Poetic fugue like the drug of you slips into me
Dylan writes of nights you've tempted to stay
A shy moon peeks at us writing of lost lovers
As you skinny-dip laughter all over my surprise.

Our deep beat slides across implied intentions
When time decides how long we play this song
You gift those electric eyes just to make me wait
I've danced with you all the days of my life, baby.

We shoulder possession's aftertaste in a new light
My eyes wander wondering if yours will ever stop
Your melancholic poetry asks me if I'll still kiss you
Visions of what might become us decide our fate.

# SCOTCH MIST

*A cold and penetrating mist verging on rain.*

## Ballet in the Rain

*A curious one*
*Stepped inside your shy rainbow*
*Granite light found us*
*A storm's ballet became us*
*As time holds onto lovers.*

# Making Unwritten Poetry Real

In the evening your vibe wants you to know
Who is still true as light ebbs leaving you now
Alone to read in between our poetic lines
Even as love spins like she wants more of you.

How do we decide how an unwritten poem lives
I touch your face as my words paint your real
Your eyes set free from time devour all of me
Each line we make up asks why you want more.

We both saunter in a pool of light making us up
By the time we remember only our eyes wait
It's as if we both have always seen what awaits
When you decide I'm real tell her you're ready.

# Light Blanketed By Our Rain


Words you wrote on my eyes still touch me
Ghostly kisses sing of when they were real
In our time of wanting, you know mine are
I hurry along these pages waiting for yours.

You found me on a day when no one knew
Stories fell across us like rain blankets in light
Lovers you had shared pieces of your heart
I puzzle them together in mirrors of us now.

Our dance along these memories never ends
It's as if your poetry wants to be inside mine
I love the way you speak of our days between
My love of everything wonders if you knew.

# Lonely Sandcastles

We crash onto shores as tides of old ghost us
Naked toes sand delight between our sunlit eyes
Poetry wonders if such waves will ever find words
Possible futures shipwreck as time abandons us.

Moontide erases steps you got used to making
Lonely sandcastles recall slipping away from us
Our metaphors in love trade secrets in new light
Each tale holds court like emotions storm inside.

Whispering in your ear the wind asks you to sigh
Oceans crawl to your bed as fervent lovers await
Their songs become a river that fires imagination
As our ghosts plead to make up these new worlds.

# Lingering Thoughts Drinking Scotch Mist

If you wear an unknown smile will anyone see you
Sassy light meanders like petulant lust wonders
We play charades between what bakes and saunters
Eyes explain everything before we decide to say.

Scotch mist surrounds an eventide tasting a kiss
Myrrh petrichor lingers on lips as a poem is born
Surprise decides to take us pretending time exists
All over mine your laughter rewrites who we were.

If I were a muse you met under these lonely skies
How would we dance as our language made us up
I've read your gorgeous mind under my moonlight
Even now as our minds smile, your light finds me.

# Anticipation's Lips


Of strange elixirs woven between her sighs
Even a charming night unveils dreams to taste
Wandering light drew pentagrams all over my surprise
Unbidden wanton thoughts lick anticipation's lips.

A taunt imagination unstuck in time reads yours
Riot heartbeats butterfly as our kettles steam
Sound awakens voices between sheets of scotch mist
Moored just offshore desire frees desperation's anchor.

Your storm windowpanes me like rain's song delights
Against a firm resolve an unrelenting atmosphere pants
No longer puzzled by our sky light floods all over us
Forgotten sighs thread tapestries into dawn's colors.

# Komorebi's Dance


I like the way you always keep me guessing
It's as if you conduct a symphony of my light
Komorebi's dance a magic you wield onto me
You forever poetry by looking me in my eyes.

Listening to something that reminds me of you
When it rains, notice that even light changes
It's as if our entanglement creates time itself
We play like children waiting to discover us.

Your smile smokes my confidence like a hug
Each time we meet a poem writes back home
I touch your face under absolutely surreal light
As a kiss imagines more, we fall under its spell.

# Seasons of Treasures

Autumnal rain waits to chill our summer heat
Leaves sigh as they wrestle with time to let go
Eyes' laughter plays in pools of leftover thought
It's as if we realize our season wants to change.

Blind against the dark shore our star ventures
We share language like a viral meme finding us
Ink decides how mine becomes yours by dawn
As words are keys, each one unlocks a treasure.

Wildwood forests beckon just as we step ashore
I look around wondering if you remember us here
Brown and green eyes dance under our rainstorm
You lead me to a meadow where empathy flowers.

# Light Eloping Under a Crescent Moon


Our pasts still dance in the solstice of our youth
Atmospheres prey on what possibilities imagine
Histories of our shadows parade as lost eclipses
Mine wants to be the blanket you use at night.

Someone spied our flowers all dancing together
In the dusky light your goddess dishevels me
Laughter spied on us as our cosmic debris reigns
Almost as if a poem might know better we join in.

Our last shy light elopes under her crescent moon
She captures everything we own even our souls
The boulevard of our haste asks if we can stay
Our spectacle maneuvers us just to remain here.

# Gardening Your Sunlight


If I garden your beautiful will your ladybugs stay?
If I hold your gaze will your wonder play with mine?
If our words lose their way should we start over?
In the time it takes us to laugh, our smiles decide.

Sunlight begging to intrude tries to kiss your lips
Lost glances run away meandering across our eyes
Time tries to catch up to our lust of entanglement
She knows all hope is lost as we step outside her.

It's a tricky moment when our threads stitch time
If our words find us here will you remember me?
If you tender love for us will our songs fly tonight?
If you flower my mind will you become them?

# Painting Poetry with Our Leftover Words

Silent words wait like unused paint on brushes
It's as if they hold our breath hostage until freed
Our sighs find valleys of inspiration and despair
Almost as if we've never met either one before.

I stir paint as words work to surface on my mind
Colors mix with my metaphors like a kiss smiles
Imagination canvases your naked pose in a word
Both of us sing about what each one does to us.

Insight envelopes our night as poetry meets paint
We listen as delicate ghosts judge what's true
Each one falls in love with a vision of what's real
My brush and mind dry now as I look for yours.

# The Haunting Melody Inside a Piano

Piano walks us through time around our naïveté
Her haunting empathetic eyes memorize our melody
Our hardwired souls sing to the electricity that rains
The flood of falling words makes us up as we go.

Her voice takes my hand shows me your empty room
Only photographs remain lining walls inside my mind
In a land where every look seems like paradise found
I can still remember that day when we were lost.

Sighs sweep past us now into the storm we became
My hand recalls yours a dance our fingers made up
Our leftover words eloquent ghosts that still tempt
Their ebbing sounds still inside us are all that remain.

## Baking Our Secret Sauce

My comfortable dark begs to taste your violin
Cognac lips drip amber onto our bold night
Our breath a cadence only desert heat can bear
We leave our bed unmade to paint what's real.

In the canopy of your eyes leftover light invites
You tried to tell me like a dream becomes true
Spring took summer and their children woke us
Confused wildness wanders across coy smiles.

Your recipe sautés as we ride our words tonight
A river of light that bakes our only secret sauce
We pin the ghost of imagination to all our futures
Your light wonders if my dark might stick around.

# Words

Words try me on as they become my thoughts
Like a ballad we might have sung about, sweet
By the time we share their stories, who are we
Does poetry mean more if they find all of yours?

Lovers mix light like lonely candles in the night
They paint their dark skies with the unspoken
When their poems find ours do you understand
Chance wonders if it's ok to sit under our rain?

We've chased dreams down strange rabbit holes
Even photographs in color masked our desires
If no one stands up for your dreams with words
Does anyone really matter when you're all alone?

# Light and Shadows in the Mist


Jazz drizzled as scotch mist poured you a drink
When somethin' else caught us together, it rained
Empathetic notes thunder like our delight dances
Your look sips my light as if the night begs for more.

Our smiles windowpane against lightning's surprise
Cannonball asks know what I mean on the flip side
Pools of emotion well in the spaces we've opened
Almost as if the music inside us is the real storm.

Darkness left alone scatters what fate never paints
In between the beauty of light and shadows we live
Even under a snowfall of winter's frozen treasures
Your song always captures my lonely imagination.

# The Language of Entangled Tears

Sadness holds eyes like love cries for a heart
Your glance captivates as mine searches for one
When we met their language an ancient secret
It speaks in tongues only poets hear in dreams.

Still in the quiet mind unfettered and seen in love
Thoughts chase down our emotional resonances
Like a lonely tear that spills out terrified by its fall
Each a magnet for yours as we dance in darkness.

Our breath a susurrous euphony in between a kiss
Almost as if each blade of sound cuts our souls
Words left alone plead to leap on lips only we open
Melancholy my sweet lover wants to hear yours.

# Butterflying Time

Torn pages butterfly away basking in leftover words
They masquerade like empathy written as time sighs
In between moments when we've traded our secrets
The look you share inside mine means everything.

Whoever you have become under these desert skies
Such vast emptiness pours into what remains of me
As time decides how we dance on our lyrical shores
Your life happens all over my soul as I write of yours.

Left in a song that cascades onto our arete'd rapport
My poetry rewrites who I am till our affinity finds us
Since all of my glances have fallen in love with yours
Our sighs write new wings for us to butterfly away.

# First Light

Your newborn deftly enlightens our awareness
She conjures up everything magnificent in us
Even before thought emerges we sense her light
Of strength in intuition's deepness we hold hers.

Conception in our poetry asks what love meant
You looked at madness to grow gorgeous wings
I remember what it feels like to be utterly alone
Thrust into a forest just to cut down my pain.

You embody a spirit who rises into each dawn
Fierce love envelopes all who ventures with you
Our dreams wander through nights like a wave
Each morning we step onto your shore in love.

## Ghostly Kisses

Rain unheeded wanders looking for lost lovers
Inside her haunted eyes sunset skies wait for us
You look to me as tears and skies mix all over us
Will you write dark poetry to me that falls in love?

Your heartbeat sings every moment you touch me
Every time we lose each other in the maddening
Like a day you spent wondering why you're there
Find your way back to me just to make the rain real.

Fearless time holds us rapt as we decide our fates
A kiss interrupted wails as if our crazy cannot stop
Tell me who are you now as my language paints us
Was I ever the poem you wanted to write all alone?

# The Haunting of Evocative Ghosts


Saint-Émilion unveiled our surprise at dusk
Visions of poignant empathy spilled our wine
Evocative ghosts and their genuine pathos
It's so hard to explain what you mean to me.

News of our remains scatter under rainstorms
I understand your flames as words I cannot say
Even as a violet sky shares her love for what is
It's a silence that surrounds me as I write you.

Stepping stones wander just ahead of us here
Imagining who we will become, words paint us
Within your charming light they story my life
As an unknown song marries our souls tonight.

# SPRING RAIN

*Spring rain is also called "latter rain;" rain that falls at the end of the rainy season which brings the grain to maturity.*

## Gardening Love

*Your happy dances like rain*
*Kissing my face*
*My eyes summertime yours*
*Gardening love.*

*Gorgeous ladybugs laugh*
*Singing your delicious name*
*Even lush forests know*
*Trees stand to hold you.*

*Flowers stretch red petals*
*Yearning for a touch*
*Such alluring delight*
*Spilling your beautiful.*

# Tousled Poetry Loves to Play on Glossy


Your tousled hair over undressed carefree lips
We'd sip morning dew on edges of coffee cups
Morning words are different creatures by night
Their gentle tentative dance at dawn awakens.

By mid-afternoon, we've traded amusing cliches
Each one asks if it's ok to jump off our glossy lips
Amusement loves to write about wild new happy
Daughter of my Calliope she gets what she wants.

Forever met us as Moon smiled eclipsing the sun
Even our delicious storms wrote together again
Our party's intoxicating mélange kissed glossy wet
We sorted out who we were just as my poem ends.

## Calliope's Glance

Too many nights wait for you to come around
They ask if I should take Calliope out to dance
She tempts me with her metaphors and similes
Even Rimbaud, Picasso, and Dylan dated her.

As I write to you tonight my mind considers us
Empty pages beg to see you between sunsets
You could say I'm a lost soul looking for love
Yet my heart remembers yours on a lonely day.

We both share smiles as if we're playing cards
Calliope's glance asks me to hurry up and come
By dawn our poetry fills skies like a cloud's rain
We all share a kiss as our music finds us again.

# Abandoned Masquerade

So we find us wanting; our laughter measuring
Asking to touch minds as everyone else falls away
Where has our poetry gone like a smile ghosts us
Crazy despair haunts eyes that we have never met.

You found me enigmatic our questions unanswered
My crazy apprehension prays for your smile to stay
Still we leave the night cold our wine untouched
As we knew not who we really wanted us to become.

From separate realities we ask uncertainty's question
A timeless wish remains sharing light under our stars
We burn just as bright as eager eyes mirror their light
Treks into such realms bridge wilder shores of love.

Abandoned paradoxes collide with our astonishment
As seemingly innocent memories tell yesterday tales
Your words fragment me as I decipher them into mine
Such labyrinthine doubts my only recourse ahead.

Skies full of possibilities as your lips ponder my eyes
Perhaps you can imagine words I create behind them
A gaze you gift kisses as we both begin another song
As ravenous desire becomes another dance partner.

Questions kept hidden in the cloud of possibilities
We've become an entangled ballet no one cuts in
Time carves us a moment to decide who we'll be
Storms gather thundering notions; after you, love?

# Melancholic Rain on Fallen Leaves

Separate realities hold us as our minds reach for yours
Words puzzle us together on days we're no longer here
Pieces of me fall away when they've forgotten their way
As light we once shared can no longer find our words.

Nostalgic dreams rake thru these fallen leaves of you
We drift back into past lives as each thought surfaces
Caught in emotional waves we drown in yesterday's
As grounded butterflies flee consuming our only hope.

Melancholic rain devours us as our surreptitious lips part
They coldly ask if goodbye still haunts in our last glance
Disguised eyes look to escape even thought has crashed
Dark secrets roam our skies cryptically clouding over us.

Perfection's challenge waits sensing we are but children
Our creativity sandboxed across entangled universes
Waking from broken dreams we paint us in tomorrow
Our emotions unveiled like autumn's golden leaves.

Spellbound we write as if our dactylic poetry defines us
Each allegory sings like a brush on canvas inspiring words
Your laugh measures us in time with amused contemplation
Every note holds my breath as your glance recaptures mine.

## A Song Unlike Any Other

It was a piano player who asked me about love
Waltz for Debby shared thoughts only for us
Sometimes your silence speaks only to me
When music touches ours poetry writes itself.

The charm of doorways meant for others fades
As my jazz refuses to become your blues, baby
Ours is a longer and patient cobblestone road
Every door we open along the way finds our real.

We met our piano player dancing with Calliope
She winked asking if we might dance with her
Your smile found mine as we all became poetry
When you're left without a song to sing, be you.

# The Stimulated Aroma of a Violet Garden

A moment's sanguine poise laid a poet's confidence
I tried to tell you of future love as our eyes took flight
Like a temple new thoughts stayed to pray for us
As they became a magnet for two entangled hearts.

Once again light across the ocean's blue wandered
Transfixed, even as we can never see inside ours
Rippled emotions play with ancient words like toys
They walk us to the shore of dawning acquiescence.

Huddled in the stimulated aroma of a violet garden
Our eyes grew new leaves of thought sipping delight
Aphrodisia danced with Calliope as our minds merged
Fever crowd-mobbed our eager tribe as we were all in.

# Distilling Our Poetic Dance

Our first words fell into time's slippery slope
Like a sacrificial dance we scored our hello's
Each line asks us how well we knew Hope
And as she beckons will you take her hand?

Atmospheres entangle what we both wonder
As darkness attempts to steal our inner light
Poets conspire to light our way under ancients
New dreams ask if we're willing to distill them?

By the time we both finish dancing, she smiles
Kindness asks all of us to enjoy a moment here
Farewells streetlight lonely walks back home
Our last words overheard as her poet winks.

# The Melody of Your Poem

So slow even a saxophone wanders as you write
A deeply touching moment stops time to stay
Eyes freed run ahead with emotional resonance
They look back at us as if they've read our future.

Your touch a jazz melody even poetry dreams of
In between a silent hush and a gasp we free words
Gifted wings, each one shares her secret then flies off
Bemused by such wonder even elvish spirits stay.

If time's illusion means language is our amber here
Poetry is the key we use to know who we'll become
As we recall days when our thoughts first began
The poem of our lives has always slowly taught us.

# Empathetic Rain

Clearly her shy ghost's eyes played with yours
Mine busy as a lost lover appeared just to dance
They escape in time but you still ghost me back
Both of us strangers in this rave of poetic music.

We sit beside thoughts playing dice in our hearts
You rain inside my mind just as a new sun is born
Our gazes mirror what we think in a bold smile
Sighs gust on tail's end of what foreshadowed us.

Stranded between what was and what could be
An angel's wings makes a sound no one has heard
The empathy of her rain startles ours to awaken
Beside myself I glance around just as you fly away.

# The Colors of Love

All the colors in my eyes paint yours like a sunset
Light streams in a breathtaking river all over them
Rain leaves poetry in your footsteps as you arrive
As if past tears follow us to remind us what love is.

Ohh, I take you down streets we still find our souls
Days have forgotten who we were as when we met
Songs we never shared come home just to be ours
All inside my words yours were the seeds I planted.

If there's a moment that made us real we kissed it
Words run ahead awestruck you might keep them
In a time when you read what such poetry means
My eyes ask if we might ever recapture such wonder?

# Mirrors of What Was and What Could Still Be

Tales of our treasured past find their way alone
Dawn's mist beckons oh to let go and fly free
To live again in the songs of youth we've saved
Oh to play in light your eyes smile just for mine.

We torched wildwood just to catch fire together
Her haunting spell still sings as each touch sears
Bathed in such charm even thought turns poetic
My eyes mirror words only your lips hold for me.

To tread the space within your heart and find us
Like meadows of light whose tides know no words
You take me there as laughter sings possibilities
Breathless and starved for you another tale begins.

# Diamond Dust

Autumnal diamond dust took us away
Just as our golden red leaves fell
We soared unlike any other then
OIur saudade hearts together.

Yet our komorebi shadows found us
As they played in between our light
I could hear your eyes tearing then
All over my words dripping from mine.

A sad susurrous breeze whispers
Your name to me like a prayer
Yet the golden light has faded now
As I remember who we were once.

# Blanketing Desire in a Dream

She asked me to dance here before I knew how
Years have gone by like words slip between lips
I've read yours as if a teacher asked me to listen
In the evening of our time now, your poetry lives.

A dark violin seeps her melancholia inside space
Perhaps it's best we'll never share the same sky
All my songs have come to remember what was
Like an old friend who blankets desire in a dream.

We took a chance one day in yesterday's mirror
Entangled in twin-flamed particles our wings flew
A poet writes about the spaces between our light
As universes branch from us, your seeds sprout.

# Our Inside Ghosts


Most of the time all of us write to you alone
We're just trying to let you hear our songs
Left in the dark words try to find your poem
But my eyes tire as only ghosts play in me.

It's not dark yet but we both love such skies
Your thoughts wander all over what I think
We've on a road without a map or a phone
I pull over just to make sure you want to be.

When highways tend to strand heartbroken
Some of us still like to breathe the searing air
I wish I knew what you still see as they leave
Ghosts of who both of us still keep inside us.

# The Days Between Us

If daybreak comes as dreams refuse to let us go
And your words still slip between our silent lips
Would you know mine as our music holds us here
Would you want me again as yours became mine?

If nightfall asks you to play these memories again
And my words fall like empathic rain erasing them
Does anything make sense when they're gone?
Should any of us question who we were before?

If dawn awakens us just to discover, should we?
I read you between what is true and what was real
It's as if we trade semantics like poker chips here
As we both wait to see whose dream still exists.

# Seduce Me Sunday

When things entangle I'm thinking of you
A pair of sly smiles winked at me tonight
I started wondering if you might know them
Almost as if everything wanted to play me.

Thoughts make us up like a fling on a cusp
Each heartbeat pleads for a sudden liaison
Passion bakes to fuck under fading moonlight
As stars start blinking like your coyish look.

You'd watch my eyes devour such delicious
Each sweet dessert loved to parade for me
I'd hold your beguile against my stone promise
Both of us falling into everything we needed.

# A Song Our Lips Refuse to Let Go

A poignant melody never requires an instrument
Just your radiant mind replaying who we are
I can see it in the way your look finds me now
No doubt we've still back in time making us up.

Your muse overslept as you dreamt of us then
She wakes you whispering her name in a poem
You can see it as a song your lips refuse to let go
She reminds you all day as ghostly lyrics call to you.

I play a record that erases everything except us
Our guardian angels play dice to decide our fate
We can see it in the way they look into us now
On a lark my saxophone cuts in and winks at you.

# Under the Dusk of Happenstance

We met in a storm sharing a similar dicey glance
Dylan wrote flowers will rise despite our rain
Your poem asks to read me under a full moon
How do we find words that make us real tonight?

I asked you to dance as we started to remember
It's too hard to be here without you in this light
They all wonder about the dancers on this floor
Another song asks if what we're doing is still real.

Under dusk of happenstance your smile sunrises
Each of us work the thread to bind what must be
If poetry has become the last road we ride home
I'll keep you in my heart as forever sunsets us.

# Quantum Doppelgänger's Dream

Twisted doppelgängers dream of our wanderlust
I met you roving a double moonlit street on Mars
Wild quantum time measures the night's disguise
Your heavy light unmasks me with a naked look.

Streetlights umbrella sobbing melancholic rain
Our eyes starved of conversation fall into orbit
Saudade tastes us meeting after we were gone
Entangled moments know where we'll end up.

# CLOUDBURST

*A cloudburst is an enormous amount of precipitation in a short period of time, sometimes accompanied by hail and thunder, which is capable of creating flood conditions.*

## Leaves of Autumn

*Precious time descends*
*Lithe diamond dust captivates*
*Seeds of tomorrow.*

# Empathy's Mirrored Umbrella

The intuitive metaphor, metaphysical riddle:
Mirrored light, all we can ever perceive of us
Sound, vibration, motion all dance together
As we move through an accelerating universe.

There's a distant shore that lies in wait for us
Treasures unmask as our forever wave breaks
We turn inward just as their truth makes us
In the darkness within, mirrors lose their way.

You and I have always met here within our poetry
We write about the stories of our shared lives
If rain has always been our empathetic riddle
Will you share yours so we umbrella together?

# Entangled Moments Like Tears in the Rain

Words you gift like unfolding petals of thought
Surround mine as they hold on to who we were
I will miss them as a new sky opens without us
Still, all of what was real keeps you in my mind.

We skip leftover stones over desolation's shores
Each one carries the weight of our lost emotions
Wonder never regrets becoming a leftover road
My dear love you touch light everywhere you go.

Our rain opens hidden landscapes no one sees
Her empathy tears as we childhood our trauma
I remember meeting you when your words held
Love was entangled moments of our friendship.

# Tears in the Rain

You, a moment time waited almost forever to unfold
I reread ancient poetry to understand your light
The tenor notes of your eyes painted inside mine
We peel oranges feeding our ravenous laughter.

Night an unbearable chill of losing you in time again
As stars enlighten us with their sweet kiss of light
Crazy afternoons writing poetry with our angels
Replenished our souls disappear as tears in the rain.

I look in memory seeing you in yesterday's shadows
Always chasing me, remaking me, wanting our real
Each time plays us all over again as they remember
Everything I've tried to leave behind as we learned.

Nipping at my heels they remind me that even now
No one ever really leaves and I can't let anyone go
Since all of our memories and shared smiles here
Last forever and will always be real under our sun.

# Sky Fires Igniting Poetry

It was eventide in my desert circumstances
My thoughts rustle as you susurrusly eye me
We trade them for another roll of ancient dice
A strawberry moon wanders between smiles.

A band sips on emotion's tide just as I say hello
Crazy sentences spark as sky fires parade by
Your laugh wraps me with hope's wry charms
Our eyes comfortable decide it's time to dance.

My heart races under the heat of raining stars
It's the passion play every desire buys a ticket
If I had any wishes left each one would be you
By midnight all that remains of us was our poem.

# Distilling Time's Vintage

Broken words live to find a light in your eyes
We run against the tide as their waves take us
Lost thoughts seek to thread us back together
Even when most abandon the light left in ours.

Poetry asks to distill our vintage across all time
Her song saunters on lips like your forever kiss
We share a sip as each word makes us up again
Leaving both of us to reinvent what they mean.

Woven emotions lead us to walk together here
Eyes of the world savour the light we both see
As evening trades a sun for a moon, love stays
We both break our words like bread for hers.

# Our Entangled Gardens

Another space flowers like your dawn thoughts
Each word you share paints us beside you here
Morning dew finds the poet in all of us awake
As if what I might pandora could make you real.

Whispers make us replay what we tried to say
I had a friend who met my naked soul and lived
Each of us an eternity flame forever entangled
Poems of us ask if anyone can feel what we do.

By eventide we both cloak desire like a flower
Yours grows in my garden as my eyes water you
Mine unleashes waves neither of us foresaw
As our passion meets, both gardens flourish.

# Your Melancholic Rain

As the evening slows and you make my eyes
A soft breeze asks us if it's time to let us go
Dylan looks back in time as fate decides us
In between our words love asks to find home.

Left all alone a complete unknown says hello
A fortune teller warms to my dark empty eyes
She weaves stories of light and love into me
As if a poet wanted you to become much more.

I've touched you when all we had was our past
You're melancholic rain and I'm stripped cold
When the sun asks if you're ready to find me
Can a future moment still bake what we had?

# Moments Raining in Our Vibe

Time changes subtly almost like eventide's light
Your eyes mirror thoughts we both trade in each
Moments seem to rain when we forget to look
Atmospheres hold onto us when we remember.

Dylan's Highlands found my muse dancing one day
We've been together there in evenings imagining
Almost as if all of us share the same vibe writing
My poems wonder if you'll ever find my shore.

Even now as I write about what's entangled in us
My words trade secrets as if language is a kiss
If we were ever to sunset time on our lonely path
Each night would make us up as our poetry does.

# Fierce Empathy

You wanted a story like our eyes always share
Even in moments when our music touches us
It's the shaking of our emotions that holds time
Their rain falls as newborn light asking for ours.

Surface tension on our lips tastes like old lovers
Their laughter songs that write poems about you
We met on shores tides love to play our games
Even as we write our poetry my eyes fell in love.

Storms within us weather this descending light
Your fierce empathy unveils our hidden stories
When I hold truth inside me yours finds me first
As if our words here have become new religions.

# Tasting Our Language

Close to the edge, we settle down on gorgeous
Descendent starlight opens your eyes in mine
We bask in illuminations from a forgotten age
Such poetry meanders as new thought devours.

We met in a fire our minds deciphered as sweet
Each line we wrote just a flavor of our yesterdays
Moments we shared here like a mirror's reflection
A taste of language no one else can understand.

You read me as words spill all over our surprise
Lips tread on them like a touch decides our fate
Freed from ancient tombs of lost literary libraries
My kiss wanders into spaces only you and I find.

# Unplayed Poetry

I had a friend who was my muse outside of time
Eternity isn't so long when we know time is short
I played our song while you disappeared one day
Poetry became our sweet lyrics to remember us.

Entangled glances never fade nor their memories
You taught me how to paint beautiful in a poem
If you can feel ebbs of our emotional waves here
How does anyone leave if time doesn't exist now?

I had a lover who wove poetry as unplayed music
Her gentle light taught me to hear yours someday
I write to you in memory of what you mean to me
Your song still harbors my heart as light leaves.

# The Hunger of an Unread Poem


Endless possibilities fly as a poem first takes flight
Dressed in your finest thoughts and memories
She dances in skies bleeding of sunsets and stars
Darkness whispers to a naked night already written.

You measure my look like an entangled lover persists
Probabilities change every time you lick your lips
Our chance overdue as each word arrives just in time
We know what's on our mind; so shall we end this?

A pregnant pause wanders in search of our silences
Evening gentles like starlight falls on a lover's pursuit
Lyrical words settle on your gorgeous like a sweet kiss
A shy moon saunters into our light reading more of us.

# Singing with Our Ghosts of Electricity

One wonders as my skies dream of your komorebi
Like stars sharing visions of your emerald beyond
Each breath we take asks whether we're real here
Under our canopy of hope only thought saves us.

There was a time we'd race against our crazy tide
Each wave seemed to know why we wanted more
When they washed over our souls only we knew it
Like a song that can dive deeper into your poetry.

There's little left on my wings as words imagine us
Almost as if no one can see who we might become
Like a dance we make without ever looking down
To be under your sky just to make our music real.

# Time as a Flower We've Always Gardened

Blues like the way we would share our moonlight
Time as a metaphor for love that asks us to be
Thought when trust is left alone without her muse
Light that never abandons us in our darkest forest.

We wrote songs as if our fever might never break
Days when a poem gave birth to another universe
Each star we visited opened our minds to others
Almost as if desire wanted to find something new.

Waves like the wind hold these thoughts together
As each moment flowers within the song you sing
I piano them just to make sure what you say is real
My fingers get lost as your eyes steal me away.

# Blues for Calliope

Cerulean hues paint my dawn blanketing lost dreams
I ride yesterday's echos remembering who I am
They thunder in my mind recalling your dark storms
Visions of future days alone knew they would come.

Haunted eyes can't escape seeing ghosted smiles
Like a lyrical voice reminding me who you once were
Morning recalls us here in her gentle lucent thoughts
They light our eyes together for yesterday's promise.

Daylight shadows me echoing such lost dreams
Summer's dulcet rainstorms reminds us of past tears
Eventide washes today as refreshed stars awaken
Mesmerized in our dance we sing her silent song.

Canopies of your beautiful light who we are now
Remembering days we couldn't stop laughter's echos
I'm holding your song sleepless across my eyes
Nights I dreamed of us till you'd look back at me.

Even when our crazy sighs pleaded to become us
Will you still remember when we're somebody else?
Obsession's deepness grips as thoughts escape
Holds me hostage as Calliope's echos color my mind.

Passion's wings sky me playing you all over again
Diving deep into possession I flee from such darkness
Cacophonies battle for light courting our skirmishes
Drenched in love, new eyes mirror what desire finds.

Sadness comforts us as thought fall into shadows
Only ghosts remain now of such resonant days
Shared beams flower like a sun-struck rainbow
They remind me of you as fires recast who we are.

Time has a way of forgetting as we embrace another
I knew we couldn't leave who we might have been
Sandstorms try to erase us as our minds distract
Your eyes bind onto mine as we never looked away.

Flights of fantasy grip us in such drowning atmospheres
Stories we've imagined wait for us like that secret kiss
Visions of what we lost tattoo torrid's foreverness
Intuition weighs hearts, yet was there ever a choice?

Breathless time measures us within a human moment
Surprise our only stop mirrored in the eyes of the night
We'd listen to a song of sighs till dawn stole our dreams
In between loss and love our scattered beautiful arrived.

Empty glass lipstick recalls branding us into the night
Stars slip in a goodbye kissing us with their shy light
The sun touches our faces as your eyes flower in mine
We speak in metaphor as a damp sky opens above us.

Rain asks if we might dance as laughter invites us in
A poetic glass of wine breaks into a surreptitious kiss
When we hunt at night shadow my voice like an echo
The moon eclipses us as your eyes make more of mine.

We read everyone like poetry to learn what they say
Even glances find delicious as we covertly bind them all
Haunting me your final look sighs as we piano goodbyes
Echoes ripple through us as terror stalks what's left.

A sudden cloudburst cries for memories we never kept
It gently sings of possibilities we'll never find again
The ebb and flow of our forever time painting us here
Just like a melody, neither one of us will ever forget.

When you're all alone now mirroring who we once were
Will you try my memory on to taste what we meant?
As tides of daylight melt into the evening's dusk
Thoughts once shared line our path like lucent gems.

Washed ashore onto this box of rain we're found
Light slips from my grasp as I am just a broken mirror
Writing to collect what remains to show your gorgeous
These words fall all out saying they were all of yours.

# THUNDERSTORMS

## Epiphany's Perception

*Seeds of thought within*
*Newborn light gasps as she flies*
*Each day thunders here*
*Your eyes an altar of love*
*Truth rains like a poem unbound.*

# Friendships Painted in Realtime

You've known me forever but we've never met
Our poetry is a kiss pages will fade over time
When our hearts decide to color us in realtime
How do I know if your canvas paints what's real?

No one knows how to rain words over us, love
Stolen moments ask to dance in leftover light
Ours is a fire only we paint between these words
Does light unveil what our treasures plead for?

My only regret is a sigh that leaves these lips
She'll never dance with words we cannot say
If poetry means that our souls wait in eternity
What should a lover do while you paint another?

# Pas de Deux

Long notes make us as we saxophone a glance
Willing fingers drum to our throbbing cadence
Pianissimos's gentle steps holds us in melody
We finding adagio's time for dawn's pas de deux.

Your rhythm carries sweet glittering sunlit smiles
We make duet delicious tasting our dolce in a kiss
Emotional torrents whip eyes tied as one in step
Musical ménage à trois delight's our soaring storm.

Our ballet allemande stirs the hunt of our lives
Heartbeat rhythms a dance only we can ever bake.
Slipping across to you a weepingly delicious ballet
As your dancing rapture footsteps all over my soul.

# La Douleur Exquise

We met under a halo of unknown dark stars
In a dream that binds lost souls through time
Enchanted la douleur exquise possesses me
Forever waiting for your command, my sweet.

Empathic skies cloud my vision of your eyes
Like a symphony no one else has ever heard
Delicate notes write of a deeper compassion
They dominate thought as does your memory.

Stillness of the night recalls immense peace
It is the way we've always known who we are
Like a piano that wanders through our minds
Your absence never leaves my thoughts alone.

# Tasting Your Electricity


It was early nightfall as you took me away
My thoughts full of those stars in your eyes
Landscapes no one else has footprinted
Like a lost lover I comply submitting to yours.

Dylan's visions reignite Mona Lisa's electricity
On the sands of our desire waves play over us
Your poems feel like delicious morning dew
Caught between our kiss and what we need.

By sunrise, smiles meet on our island universe
A taste of you breakfasts what we both dream
Entangled breath laughs at our quantumness
Love tired of waiting to dance storms our eyes.

# The Epiphany of Poetry in a Rainstorm

An unseen poet's wings carries her soul
Into vast architectures of a wondrous realm
We met building sandcastles in rain clouds
The love affair of a poet and her imagination.

Like a kiss you only see in a dream she smiles
Lost words take flight as eyes touch her wings
Epiphanies storm your wild as she looks back
Would you like to fly with me to tame our poem?

Complex light asks if you really know her mind
She reads yours like empathizing rain in a storm
Wonder gardens our minds as if we just met
Our wings take us to a place only poets recall.

# Tempting Our Tempestuous Nature

Demur like a shadow on the moon's face
Your smile.
Our eyes protest in the loneliness of time.
My thoughts a forgotten samba waiting to cut in.
A hot sun rains rivers of us just as you bite your lip.
I smile back losing track of who's leading our dance.
Synchronized lips wonder if we'll ever give in.
A moment beguiles us with our last memory.
As the music begins again.
A sigh enraptures.

# Riding Our Madness On a Wave

You would ask me when do we ever come ashore
The rivers of light have no conscience as we ride
Between thought and passion we surf our lives
Today I could taste your laughter like those waves.

I remember the time you became so much more
We'd listen to music as our madness took flight
Even when we were all alone it never stopped
You knew what was happening as we went down.

Dried roses line the hearts that plead for our past
In the evening of a passion play we play our cards
Will your song still ask me to dance as we leave
My poems wander all across the last look you gift.

# Our Dragons Soar in Forever Light

Seemingly alone light wanders lost remembering us
A luminous moment saved because we became it
Memories of lost love songs wrapped inside us
Do you still keep that day as a fire upon our deep?

Chills play within my heart  as flames consume us
We knew our dragons live soaring in forever light
Luminous thought always rises to each occasion
As lucid dreams awaken as our wings unfold them.

Komorebi's light surreptitiously asks if you'll play
She invites our eyes to find ourselves before we go
All your glances mirror everything I've seen in you
A sudden shared hug pleads to recall these words.

## Imaginary Shores

We move as if our shadows know where to go
As Sol sets behind us they run ahead laughing
Unknown rain cuts in to dance with everyone
In the desert, light bends what stays inside us.

Difficult choices storm as we play dealt cards
Tired eyes realize there's no place like home
A poem is born as yours make peace with mine
Could we be someone different under the sun?

Love means nothing unless you can wear me
On the lonely shores of our imaginary deserts
I have always kept a candle lit just for you
When our shadows kiss again hold me tight.

# Echoes

Words met us alone so many years ago
They wander now as we dream of them again
Memories in the cusp of yesterday's twilight
Each one a candle in your eyes of desire.

# Favors

A play we forever in our lightness of being
Chills write my words like marks of desert rain
Their waves ripple through my thoughts of you
Echos dance in my mind as you leave with them.

# Desire's Sunsets

Dawn sautés our dreams as we breakfast time
Smoking her stark light we bend space to smile
Your laughter spanks mine as both of us eat
Suddenly the promise of what's in store invites.

Sonoran heat blends ours in a seared oven bake
Delicious rain asks if you're thirsty for my sweet
In dying sunlight both of us meet desire's sunset
Whatever we do now plays us like another dream.

We slip into eventide like a crescent moon rises
Her nascent light a stealthy kiss we both share
She washes empathy over our eyes like sun rain
Stars emerge as both of us fall in love with her.

# Gates of Delirium

We breakfasted with Coltrane over easy at dawn
trees crowd around us sighing supreme in song
adroit light dances in leaves as lissome skies loiter
On a lark, your temptation conquers dear Prudence
As the silence of eyes contemplate a new thought
We storm our gates of delirium just as rain steps in
Petrichor steeps within us just to cool the madness.

Sipping euphoria's breath our frozen thoughts fly free
Ghosts of nocturnal raves simmer in sudden delight
Wonder's vibe asks to slip desire between your lips
We saunter into familiar as brazen takes our wheel
Rapture never waits for license in the well of a kiss
Delicious time seizes what's real in our naked truth
Your fire consumes us as we sculpt coy au revoirs.

## Sharing My Wings with Yours


Adrift on a sea of chaotic thoughts we set sail
No shore is too distant, we think at light speeds
A calm wind reminds me you are searching too
Our wings catch as we both hold what matters.

In evening as light begins to fail you come to me
Darkness tempts as her poet charms everyone
Dusk asks me whether to go or to stay with her
You own me like a sunrise takes the night to bed.

Scattered rain plays new thoughts as if we knew
Poetry you gift becomes a storm thought needs
Mine gathers us as your wings take hold of me
In sudden light we both know how to find home.

# Dancers Always Seek Similar Light

If time replays our light I will see yours again
When does a dance ever forget a song shared
As we measure honor, fate, and even love here
Daring skies reimagine what they make us feel.

Rimbaud, Picasso, and Dylan sought out reality
Abstract reasoning crosses between our ethos
Like the time we both understood who we are
A moment without you captures my soul, love.

Reasonable minds live in time on a chessboard
Thought may decide fate as we move closer
I met you once before we knew who we were
You played me as a master who loved to dance.

# The Unwritten Poetry of Rain


Blues for a divinity of rain in the human desert
Mirrors reach into you to see your architecture
In a life of reflection even light doesn't know
Does a poem unveil what's beyond your look?

Caravans of our mysterious roam universes
Each shore we crest holds pieces of our soul
Your time alone wrote a blueprint for beautiful
As we all fade in time, your light never does.

Prophets of desire a study we render in music
Words become islands of awakening as we sing
I read your eyes like impatient unwritten poetry
When you touch my hand her rain makes us.

# CORONAL RAIN

*Coronal rain is created by plasma that expands up a magnetic loop that extends from the sun's surface. The plasma gathers at its peak, and as it cools, condenses. Gravity then pulls the plasma back down the loop which then rains onto the Sun's photosphere.*

## Rhapsody in Your Rain

*Words rain within us*
*They find ours as we delight*
*Each one a tiny seed*
*Gardening love in our minds*
*Into the song of ourselves.*

## Sunglassing Yesterday's Surprise


Bopping inside you spill soporific smiles like champagne
They're all over my surprise even your demure peeks out
Laughing our drowsy footprints wander just behind us
They mingle all over each other knowing where we're at.

Delight asks if you're real curious if you'd taste my lips
She knows me so well; laughs at all my inside jokes
Your eyes sunglass me as they saunter all over mine
We know why we're here mirroring light into smiles.

You've haunted me like newborn flowers crying in rain
They hold my eyes inside yesterday's hypnotic dreams
I inked your farewell card listening to Melancholy
Just to tell you someday what I couldn't say today.

Sandcastling our moments, time crashes around us
As if nothing is real even my surprise has become yours.
Champagne we never tasted, just hopeful glitterati eyes
Poetry pens a sanguine future as our song fades away.

# Our Empathic Storms

There were times I couldn't recognize you, love
Angry within a rain that dissolved who we were
Caught outside of time we lost our touch today
Laughter suddenly reminds us who we've been.

Abandoned masquerades linger like night's allure
A new shore opens beckoning who we could be
Wonder masks desire as if we're childhood lovers
I catch glances you fire as if you're ready for me.

Candlelight spills over empathetic windowpanes
Our eyes share license to hold onto rain's embrace
In a moment of silence, our storms wander away
You put your arms around me as our eyes dance.

# Beneath Rationale's Surface

Profound dread triggers distant echos within your mind
Once you begin to follow them they keep you there
Darkness takes a hand as you both embark into time
Thoughts collide over your loss; recourse has left you.

Blindsight envelopes what reason has forgotten to share
In sixty seconds you've relived twenty-one years past
Body-quakes ripple across your skin like waves on water
Coherent deduction asks the price you're willing to pay.

Emotional quicksand refuses all your bribes to let you go
In between imagination's skies and realities you breathe
The chilling phone marks you with sudden hope and fear
All you can translate is "Your daughter is safe."

# Desperate Chances

Loss for words, a poet resurrects yours to write
Nonplussed, you share time as a new language
My deadpan astonishment races to invent words
As the night gets heavy, sentences get shorter.

Dylan's music encourages our desire's bravado
We meet under Saturday's desperate chances
Her light becomes a spellbound dance we relish
Like songs that play on our lips we kiss her hello.

You take hold of me as if she might steal my soul
Darlin' I'm not going anywhere, so look into me
Treasures you find are yours corridoring my mind
Each poem I write touch deeper inside yours.

# Ghosts of Tomorrow's Fires

Silent rage races like rain against windowpanes
Thought lost across a forest of uncharted futures
Rises like steam searching for a cauldron of hope
Poured our wine just to calm my seething unrest.

Truth is crucified as if her likeness never mattered
Fear of retribution sleeps with each lost soul here
When you imagine a dream to make life beautiful
Do tomorrow's ghosts come home as you awaken?

Love wanders as we debate who should make us up
In the evening of our lives she asks if you remember
All of our secrets spill out as we decide each future
In the end I will hold you close as the fires become us.

# Burning in Your Daring Light


Underneath thought our charm sizzles in wait
Appetites conspire with emotional resonances
Holding court their ménage à trois challenges us
Avenues of desire streetlight what we both need.

Social media rolls up her Saturday welcome mat
Depeche Mode plays *Love Thieves* just for us
Will your daring light still burn so brightly tonight?
My poem turns as I'm hungry and it's time to eat.

Sweet damp sheets envelope another war and peace
We write history as if our melancholic fears rule us
Each sigh gifted I candle yours just to make us last
Our sunsets refuse to date, so we begin again.

# Making Up Our Own Rules

Day finds thought bound to who are we apart
Minds work to wrap us up yet we cannot be boxed
Dreaming we fall into skies roaming distant stars
Haunted by yesterday, pleading for tomorrow.

Night finds thought's alone moments lost in time
Searching and grieving will we ever awaken Dawn?
Still moving through light, time's hold long forgotten
Our laughter reaches back into who we once were.

Ancient gods taught us how we might play here
Making up new rules as your fire rekindles mine
Rising across vast skies I measure gorgeous eyes
Lost within your dark, can you remember mine?

I map your words as a road ahead pockets my steps
These days the moon's waning darkness tempts me
You walk ahead alone leaving such days behind us
Reminding all we made still glints across our paths.

We follow deep-felt words measuring heart's lament
Singing them together we'd polish our lost shadows
When the eventide beckons onto our shores, love
Find my words written behind your eyes; never lost.

# Decoherence

Schrödinger and Heisenberg loved our pets
Their uncertainties blush entangled moments
Your eyes make us up as if we're only on tv
Time's waves decide if we can still be seen here.

Labyrinthian thoughts fly skies for desert minds
I try to write to them yet your memories escape
They take us apart as we wane in ebbing light
Eloquent glances our only recourse to reappear.

Sanguine emotions flood as melancholia bonds
Poignant hunger beckons in tomorrow's rain
Light entangles my poet's dark doppelgängers
As their music seduces me to write about yours.

Our decoherence now invites angels and ghosts
Starlight falls through us like quantum particles
I feel your glance as a ripple painted in our time
Darling, what has become of our kittens?

# Your Wings Like Poems in the Rain

The rain holds all of me as if it's my glue here
I rage against our storms knowing they free us
When these words fall onto you do they matter
It touches me like I loved yours dripping all over.

Alone l am now accustomed to her cold embrace
I play music to find out who you are in the night
It's as if we've always known how to open doors
Yet our mysterious natures ask us to go so slow.

I'm ready to abandon what has already left me
There's a rush in a snowstorm that's never cold
I was a lost soul before you found a light with me
My days open new poems waiting for your wings.

# Being Us in the Rain

Whispers of rain found us as our song took flight
We wore her cloak like an entrenched melody
Each line dug deep into what we had once buried
All along strange shores where tides erased us.

Thunder shouted out in search of dark company
Somber storms rainbow'ed over our imagination
In the ebbing of another day, our light fades away
Solitude casts a plea for the intimacy of eyes.

Sunlit expressions dawn in a shower's splendor
Her poetry washes over those waiting for smiles
When I write about you even the rain debates me
Yours falls as if we both want to feel more of it.

# Splintered Sunlight

Our hands make us walking in splintered sunlight
Bodies that slip in between komorebi's delightful
Minds so utterly voracious even thought enflames
Your glance a scotch mist enveloping my crazy fire.

Sun lights on gorgeous landscapes holding breath
A shared smile touches me in a place only you go
As we inch our way through yesterday's dreams
Who can say what might become of these sighs.

On a day when trees let go of their leaves, we met
Diamond dust streets our steps like time doesn't
Hearts find their way as if no one knows our name
Your gentle rain forevers music of a lover's taste.

# Dragons of Desire

Sixty-four quadrillion conscious entanglements
As your eyes drop down into my next thought
We sleep measuring our possible probabilities
Awakening, everyone remakes them over again.

Dragons of desire reimagine who we need to be
The poet becomes you as our song sings to us
You know I will remember ours even as we leave
Uncertainty wonders like a cat left outside time.

I've traveled inside your mind and you felt me
A glance unlocks each treasured enlightenment
We bake our overthinking as the teacher waits
Her patience softens as love flings us back.

# A Poet's Quest

Our eyes hunting under candlelight's quest
As if desire knew us before our fire started
Warm ash bespeaks our night's questions
Like love's intensity blanketing what's left.

Pages pursuit us like a poet imagining yours
Words steal away breath as we inhale them
In between what you mean, mine remains
Like a fire still searching for your candle.

Your language makes me up in dark poems
Jupiter's eclipsed moons all dance in delight
Almost as if both of us write outside of time
Our eyes lock as we light up what we want.

# Our Words

Our silence thunders without your eyes on mine
Even as moonlight wanders between sly smiles
Where her magical song asks us both to dance
Under skies we call home yours is always mine.

Our laughter speaks of everyone we've ever met
Poets conspire to make up what we both share
We move into each other as our music holds us
Each time your fire begins mine forgets who I am.

Our moment waits till both of us learn who we are
All these words feel like our blood rushes inside
You've got stars in your eyes and they all find me
Every night your memory sleeps in these dreams.

# Giving Up Our Ghosts to Write Poetry

We've never reconciled differences we play upon
Just let them make us over like a new poem does
Always it's words both of us saved as treasures
You know it's true as silence becomes a love song.

Skies flow over us as they remind us of our pasts
Places we would learn how to love what's inside us
You can feel it as strangers look at you wondering
Always it was in our eyes that gave up our ghosts.

Did you ever realize who I was behind these words
Just another poet who found you caught in the rain
We learned how to say hello in different languages
Even now as you're a memory writing who we were.

# SNOWBURST

*A snow burst is a very intense shower of snow, often of short duration, that greatly restricts visibility and produces periods of rapid snow.*

## Seasons of Friendships

*Under Winter's moon*
*Friendships reign like snowfall's bliss*
*We recall our thrill*
*Snowmen guard our lonely gates*
*Even the desert mountains.*

## Envelopes of Time

January awaits as she bakes us in her icy beds
Ansermet's *Nutcracker* shades in our delicious
A ballet across our decembering temperaments
As our steps slide into histories only we recall.

Tastes of friendships linger as time wets our lips
We wonder as our dance makes us as if we're real
Days when all we can find is your beautiful words
Light surrounds me here conspiring to let you go.

Left alone a soul still finds her time to become us
Like butterflies caught in an empathetic rainstorm
Their wings lift us all encased in effervescences
Envelopes of time written onto our mirrored eyes.

# Making Your Poetry Real

When you walked into your real and knew it
Each one you met shared her smile knowing
All you ever need is a love you've always made
She's your spirit as her words make you here.

When you go away sunflowering all over mine
Tastes of your light seep into me like my rain
Each kiss that wanders on such roads remains
Like a moment haunts both of us through time.

We've known us forever yet we've never met
Like a poem that has no beginning or end here
Each line you share asks me to find my next
As I walked into my real and recognized yours.

# Songs Only We Can Play

Candlelight asks if our poetry means anything
Our language a flame here in and out of minds
Words prepared like opulent delicious recipes
Each one we hold in our lips like a forever kiss.

Under rain, a look takes us both back thru time
Almost as if our storms knew what would work
I rewrite my song for you every sunrise, lover
Between lonely words, spaces wait for yours.

Favorites ask if we should play them together
You write poetry no one deciphers till night falls
Mine has become waves we only find when lost
Have both of us written songs no one will sing?

# Deepness Distilled

I was an unopened bottle aging for your first taste
As time embraced me my patience longed for you
You kept me laughing when sharing another's love
Deepness distilled waiting till I came of age for you.

Gardens flourished within us as we seeded futures
Seeds of what we'd become planted other histories
Till one day you found me and I opened up for you
Only our poetry remembers now what we found.

You were a glass of light waiting for our stars to fill
We met on a night both of us fell under their spell
Magicians conspire to weave the love that we think
By the time you read my eyes, I was already gone.

# Our Gorgeous Bare Trees in Winter

Beginnings' sweet moment as another universe opens
You step into a new real slipping into both of them
Dawning realization fills silence as light blossoms
Secreting uncertainty like empathic rain on our lips.

New music captivates as you play across your mind
A seamless blend becomes you unifying universes
Wrapping your words inside me they dance in mine
Mesmerizing what's left they show me how you feel.

When you're alone find mine strewn in leftover light
Look for me inside them as they play for our souls
When you've forgotten days we'd laugh and cry
Tell me what I was when you were once my poem.

Tranquility becomes us as we riding our rogue waves
Summer eloped with autumn loving our bare trees
I miss your sunstruck eyes like you painted everyone's
Mine komorebi'd as I step into another memory of us.

Desert skies embroiders our serene light together
They rain on us feeding on strange moonlit nights
Words harvest us like a sun flowering at night
Haunting glances keep as I garden my thoughts.

Silence owns our time as we breathe the scent of us
Atmosphere'ing passion through timeless moments
Within dream's wreckage only poetry can remember
Love whispers thought like a shore only we footprint.

# Lost in Our Cherished Enigmas

Capricious looks penetrate baking inside our minds
Abandoned masquerades unveil new horizons
Singing electric now we lingua franca time
Dialect'ing secrets creating our prized enigmas.

Washed ashore like bottles we free us at dawn
Fervidly butterflying cherished light's bijoux
Rain cries for memories that we've lost as sighs
Almost like a melody we've always tried to recall.

Cold breath gets inside unraveling our pasts
Wondering were we real, will the temptress awaken
Surreptitious lips own time conspiring against ours
Her forever look a sly smile only she can handle.

Rain loves to find us alone as she waits to be real
Washing what's true leaving us in our naked light
If you touch me like her, would you mirror mine
Wake me in your light as you piano my sad smile?

Gently playing a forever flow we paint us here
Upon each moment as if we might never leave
I've always held on to our captivating first dance
Joy that still resonates like thunder in the rain.

Stories we've left behind sweet muse of my words
I fell in love with yours bending time in our light
We are still just unwritten poems trying to find us
You gifted me words as they fell in love with yours.

# Drinking Songs Like Wine

Your music and light a deepness shared with us
Ballads thread our lives together weaving words
We'd get drunk on their verses dancing in your rain
Time leaves us faded holding on to what they mean.

I'd write about you painting words in your skies
We'd drink songs like wine kissing time goodbye
Visions of a night's couplet dreamed us into dawn
Madrigal vibes sunrise as we taste who we were.

Sleeping alone our music has changed who we are
When you read my eyes does your poetry find you?
In the dusk ink of our thoughts paged across yours
Who makes us real when everyone's chorus fades?

# Passion's Remains

A blue moon steals secrets like my imagination
Lovers wait till their silhouettes paint us over
Under her midnight komorebi shadow, a smile
As if you know exactly what my poetry means.

I wanted to find you searching for my dreams
Like a poet digs graves for what passion leaves
I've danced with you for so long I've forgotten
Days you and I made love all over both of us.

Tomorrow night slips her ghost into our desire
Words sleep with all of us as we make us up
We've never met yet I know about your smile
Secrets both of our souls have always imagined.

# Our Gravity

Your silence ghosts me like Dylan wonders
Each time mine speaks up we play us again
When time asks if our moments are still true
Only what we share matters in what's left.

Each word in your poem gives you up to me
Their dance asks if what we shared was real
Gravity slips between everything we ask for
Only when a mind touches us do we exist.

Who do we become when no one else cares
It's a question we envelope as we disappear
Our thoughts keep asking to dance with you
Your voice awakens mine as we both wonder.

# Dancing with Our Darling Ghost Stories

A rogue dragonian thief begs to steal your eyes
Her sweet smile basks on those scoundrel lips
Like an evening tries to cut in as we look away
Coy saunters onto us like a desperado's knife.

Just in time, the band plays *Blues for Calliope*
Her sister Melancholia hijacks reason's pleads
Sudden laughter reigns as we flash mob desire
As outlaw lovers scandalously take our hands.

The game's afoot as no one dancing looks down
Even Dylan's tunes know better to stop us now
Our darling bandit cooks up new ghost stories
We kiss her eyes farewell as they all become us.

# The Haunted Eyes Behind Desire

I've seen your eyes laughing in the pouring rain
They knew so much more about what's coming
We would skip like stones across the waterfall
Anyone who saw our happy piper'ed behind us.

Our alluring race became a storm, a lightning rod
We stepped out flaunting our real like hard rain
Days between what we wanted and what we lost
Have turned our words from promises to regret.

Echoes play across our minds like those stones
Their path still unknown until we realize it's ours
In the evening's ebbing hold, a dream resurfaces
Haunted looks escape from what desire decides.

# Treasuring Light

December'd like a snowstorm that wrote poem one
Days pass through memories we shared in winter
Passion drips her intuition within us as our ice melts
I used to send you calligraphic letters from my heart.

A sunless cold still breaths on snowbound streets
All these years have passed, only ours has changed
I remember when we first met; music has our souls
Hold my hand again just to say hello as we return.

Ohh, the delicate sound of your name like a song
Each time I replay them each moment holds me
Like falling snow capturing this imagination now
You've always been light that both treasure here.

# Metaphorical Visions


Whisper to me everything you write in my eyes
Our ghosts serenade as light pours in our souls
Inside my words your heart wraps my intention
All of these visions ache for remembered skies.

You take my smile in a glance that never lets go
Even as my mind metaphors all these thoughts
Rimbaud, Picasso, and Dylan handed out Love
Their language still makes what's real in our night.

We trade heat for everything that emotions stir
A lonely kiss dances for attention in a full moon
When you take mine all of our spirits disappear
Beside myself, I write what you've gifted to me.

# Ocean Anchors

The way glances dance like rain on ocean waves
You feel heartbeats skipping like stones on you
Like a drum beat none of us want to escape from
Dressed in short blue jean cutoffs we both dive in.

I wanted to light your candle just to see my surprise
Words dripping of ghosts we both still sleep with
Each sound spins on a carousel we saved in time
Don't you wonder what I'm like reading my poem?

Your electric vibe reminds me of Calliope's charm
In between songs, my thoughts reconstruct you
Like Miles or Beethoven might copy your deep vibe
When it's time to pull up anchor and sail, take me.

# Calliope's Eyes

Lyrical notes help me find your lost vision, love
They excavate passion's blindness as we sing
Inside the poetry of a glance, Mona Lisa sighs
We cut in to dance as everyone shares a smile.

A shy sky wanders across our surprise like stars
The sudden moment pleads as even light fades
In between days when we would paint ourselves
Our language reimagines how nightfall takes us.

Calliope's eyes ask whether or not we should be
A poem plays to all of such passionate thoughts
We stop them in their tracks just to kiss her hello
Her smile a storm of what love bakes, bids adieu.

# Komorebi's Poetry

Eventide descends almost like music can envelope
I consider you here as I extrapolate your new poem
Everything is quiet as eyes storm like empathic rain
My words let loose ask if your gaze will make mine.

By the time we replay sentiments, time has left us
We surmise a sunrise just like our smiles ask hello
You write poetry mapping light's magical komorebi
Even draped shadows behold how we'd together.

My heart tides like an Aberdeenshire ocean wave
Footprints beach onto our souls as we touch down
You study them as they lead back to when we met
By the time our eyes meet again we both know us.

# Flowers For a Lonely Poem

I dreamed of you in a poem one lonely night
The stars huddled together over sky's mirror
Eerie mists carried your sweet lyrics to me.

Melancholic saudade rain flowering in gardens
Starlight's gentle komorebi rays
Your petrichor delightful myrrh on my lips
Mnemosyne's epiphany as I remember us
Calliope's kiss as I finish my poem for you.

Dawn's awakening unmasked such memories
As language only you and I could share
Like a lonely poem dreams for your sweet eyes.

# PETRICHOR

*Petrichor is a  distinctive, earthy, usually pleasant odor that is associated with rainfall especially when following a warm, dry period and that arises from a combination of volatile plant oils and geosmin released from the soil into the air and by ozone carried by downdrafts.*

## Your Rain

*Your rain arouses*
*Petrichor surrounds our souls*
*Komorebi seeks us*
*Turbulent waves search our shores*
*Shared kindness sandcastles us.*

# Dancing Inside Our Shadows

I met your heart in the wild desert of my mind
She knew exactly what I needed to hear
The wild mountain fire winds carried her voice
Just like when we would sing the song of you.

When I close my eyes, darling you still make me
Lost thoughts saxophone all over who we were
In between what we saved our poetry became us
When my eyes made yours we disappeared.

All the younger lovers smile when they see us
I think of the time when I looked thru their eyes
A radiant sun always dances inside my shadows
Just like the days when you would meet me here.

# In the Evening of Our Lives

Been in Cali so long I find sunsets inside of you
Atmospheres painting silent melodies above us
In the land of mountains and oceans our air sings
As again we all walk through times of love and loss.

The razor blade of time asks if our healing has set
My emotions lay asunder pleading to find you now
Lost thoughts scamper like a newborn happiness
All of them play with our souls as we touch down.

Chills envelope us in time to the look in your eyes
It's as if each word is a gift we can never forget
Like a sunset that tries to heal what the day shared
Will you remember them when my memory fades?

# Wandering Footsteps on Pebbles and Sand

This road finds our footsteps silently wavering
They're sharing a dream we've only seen once
Pebbles and sand wander away as thoughts fly
Even as our sound fades love surrounds them.

Peace invites us to table what we're meant to be
I met yours once when all I had to share was me
Storms crowd my skies now as words befriend us
You were always here when the rain took me away.

There's a longing between these steps we share
A cadence that settles in our bones as we dance
It's almost as if our lives have always made love
Moving together in the song only we sing here.

# Of Poems We Have Become

Music's notes our thoughts and emotions consume
Chills ripple across ghosts our bodies still hold dear
As we use language's own cantata to become us
Each song you share reinvents who I thought I was.

Spellbound both of us simultaneously find epiphany
Her awakening feels like your sunrise over my night
Electricity runs through my words as I imagine them
Each one touches yours like a waltz we'll never finish.

If poetry is indeed music held within our eternal souls
Yours touches mine as if they dance together in time
All these roads we've shared with our precious words
Seem as metaphors for us to become such poems.

# The Bibliothèque of Our Souls


Our time dissolves as sacred pages in bibliothèques
Moments you gift share tales in sacrosanct palimpsests
Poetic rain opens a much-loved scene as I look at yours
Even in a storm light binds in eyes holding on for life.

A hundred memories plead for charms you bestow
They capture a part of you that slipped alway in them
The library of Earth overflows with our gorgeous souls
As oceans rewrite lost fables into tomorrow's dreams.

Splintered sunlight windows past dust and cobwebs
Mirrors confuse who is the reader and who is the story
Bound up in our minds love searches for interpretation
Such a short time to play our lives, who will remember?

# Poetic Waves

Days have fallen in love with years in our time
Friendships come and go, yet here we remain
And the wind let me go sighing like a wild rush
We'd soar into tomorrow, our poetry making us.

Distant shores beckon holding our footprints
Waves laughed with us composing their poetry
Who we are now remembers what they mean
Different skies, yet our words are always real.

We've danced around the sun again, mon chou
Only few have shared her light as you do
As sun, moon, and stars all fell in love with yours
And the sky rains about you stealing my breath.

## Our Cherished Enigmas

Ardently, we wonder of your sweetness darkened
Acoustic words, keys we use to open perception's door
It's a silent metamorphosis written across intent eyes
I conjure up words strewn like music within my mind.

We find purpose hidden behind such longing moments
Such is our light we find when we read you in our time
Whimsical tastes penetrate as they bake inside all of us
A dance we've scored deepening our trusted memories.

Singing electric, I lingua franca who you might be now
Dialecting secrets we invent our own cherished enigmas
Washed ashore like vintage bottles, we break dawn
As fervid butterflied embraces euphorically take us.

# Leaving Possible Entangled Envelopments

A change of plans now as you're not the one
I was the fun you had even in our crazy laughter
Friendships metamorphosize who we might be
Until mutations fall off the cliffs of lost smiles.

When you're left alone apart as our song ends
What were you thinking of in your empty space
You rewind everyone looking for failure's truth
Strange tales of your intuition spells their doom.

All of our sweet endless entangled envelopments
They dance in our reach as others eye to cut in
When your darkness abandons who am I left with
Should mine fall apart in your lingering shadows?

# Ghosts of Summer

August days burn to stretch our fading memory
As we'd huddle together with Summer's charm
Thought reaches out cleansing walls of my mind
Making space for the golden leaves of autumn.

Her diamond dust binds with a deeper resolution
As I bury our past echoes; a song I once loved
We all replay them just to remember such ghosts
Jewels of thunder and rain will always recall yours.

Bold September waits as we change our clothes
New pieces of who we wait to become emerge
Whatever is past now free, is alone to take wing
As we all take flight to find our new way home.

## Sleeping with Lost Time

Rain met us as her eyes locked down onto ours
Blind for a moment I recognized your reflection
Torrid emotions play in between moistened light
Tearing you realize my poem isn't about yours.

We shared lessons umbrella'ed under social skies
Each write soared temptations to play this game
Children of an ancient age all of us know our way
Yet is it chance that entangles what we all desire?

Most of my friends have fled these silent spaces
I sleep with time wet with their fading memories
Your name invites me as a dance asks to happen
It's clear our song ended before we said goodbye.

## Catching Smiles

Your sound takes both of us into an abyss
Electric ghosts fracture time into moments
Sanity breached by a look no one waits on
We walk through a lens made only for us.

Catch your smile as we both laugh relieved
Last night remembers more than either of us
I wrote a poem standing outside your door
My words kept knocking between us all night.

Wonder reminds me of all your temptations
Left alone with our imaginations our eyes sing
Till time decides if either of us becomes real
We save our souls by making us up each day.

# Lover's Wings

Cold wind masks our dreams tonight
Answers wait till both of us awaken
Don't let this chill take your heart
We both write over lost memories.

You look at me, a kindness holds us
Each word we share makes us up
Even our myths wonder who we are
Till love reaches out to ask hello.

My eyes wet as we both say farewell
Only in our poems do we really dance
A lover's wings waits till you're ready
Between what was and what is we live.

# Deconstructing Dreams

Sometimes when your words catch mine we fly
Leaves scatter all along our autumnal passions
Hungry for their lost trees and the fertile ground
They dance trading old light for what we'll dream.

When everyone looks away as we share what's us
Our words slip between poetry we both make up
Tangled all along what we first thought was real
You touch down rushing all over my empty pages.

Left untouched our metaphors ask if we're still ok
As if a poem might deconstruct who you could be
I write to you listening as heartbeats hold my pen
Almost as if what you dream conjures up my own.

## Poetry that Decides What We Might Think

I started a poem overthinking about who we are
Words asked me out all day as I thought of you
Each one touched us both as they danced in me
Almost as if we have known each one all our lives.

This one finds tears as Calliope's wings descend
She knows how to make time become what's lost
Surreptitiously who we once were wears our hearts
Your look asks if I want to fly one more time again.

In the evening of our poem we find our metaphors
They surround us within astonished atmospheres
Each rhetorical sigh paints us back into a moment
You finished my poem reminding me who you are.

# Descending Starlight

Your gentle rain falls onto my petrichor soul
Leftover light spills from our eyes as we fly
An eerie blue moon plays your favorite jazz
Sighs embrace us like a lost sunset found again.

We dance to our unwritten song on midnight ink
Your thoughts bask under descending starlight
I write poetry that imagines everything can fly
Our wings settle suddenly as Dawn plays for us.

Clouds bereft of heavy burdens invite us to soar
Sky full of imaginations dreams of what's real
Your lips circle this poem as if my words can kiss
We bed our minds with thoughts of what's true.

## A Farewell Like a Gorgeous Sunset

I found a magical soul in our tides like a rare gem
Even now as only waves remain I sense her touch
Like many others we never spoke or shared light
Yet the language of poetry became our home.

Words scatter over my page now as I think of you
They're entangled with what we've left behind us
Each stop along our way another one held on dear
As they fade emotional resonances linger on lips.

Only a loving heart dives into an unknown ocean
Such fate is true for those who trust themselves
When you swim with such enchanted creatures
Look for a smile that reminds you of our magic.

# The Secret of Stopping Time

Pandora stepped on my toes in our forever dance
Your smile painted emojis all over my restraint
Like a poem you still decipher her new languages
Wonder awaits as we both lose ourselves in the song.

A piano walks us hand-in-hand back to the bar
Subtle changes have taken my inner voice tonight
We read much more in our absence than in our words
It's not who I am as much as it's about who we were.

I've thought of you today under our changing light
Each moment we trade secrets, time stops for us
As if we move back and forth between possibilities
Our future's still entangled between what we might decide.

# EPILOGUE

*All poems never really end*
*Yours distill light I have only imagined*
*We share time as if our poetry moments still matter*
*when we're gone.*
*Be the words that you share*
*when nothing else remains.*

It was you wasn't it on that crazy day when everything seemed to have a deeper meaning and our poetry wrote itself like a rainstorm that still had something to say before the sun decided it was time to roll our dice again, right? Did you notice that such poems are the ones that have never left us even as those days have become memories both of us have put away as treasures we can't afford to lose?

We are all much more than the poetic embers that still burn brightly in our minds and hearts after the last line is written. Heed the fact that even behind the words of a romantic melancholic poet, the seas are intensely chaotic and like all of our voyages into uncharted waters, islands of reason and emotion lie in wait for us to anchor and explore. We are all storms in pursuit of a shore to land upon and become the rain that empathizes who we dream about becoming tomorrow.

It's a night when a poet meets herself in our sea of possibilities and language changes the game for everyone who reads what's left once the words find root inside our own. It's as if we first imagine you in black and white on a canvas and the colors we find inside your soul enable us to create the poem that's always been waiting for us to let it out so its wings can soar.

If a poet writes about the life you've lived in some manner and she asks you if her work made you dive down deep to discover things that you perhaps have left in yesterday's mirrors as time has made you move on in different circles, how does her poetry make you feel when you realize that you're the poet and each and every poem you've written means more to us than anything we've ever read before?

## Lost Chances


*We used to write across lost vanities*
*They would hold our fires like ghosts*
*I'd open your look into words we knew*
*You took mine as if they were our last.*

# ABOUT THE AUTHOR

Verde Mar began writing enigmatic, romantic, and melancholic micro-poetry just as the global pandemic began. He was born in Rhode Island, just off the Wampanoag Trail by the Narragansett Bay. Earning a bachelor's degree in computer science at New Mexico State, Verde began a career in technical writing in the San Francisco Bay Area. He designed and built a home by the ocean in Half Moon Bay as his family welcomed twins onto our little blue-white box of rain just to keep busy like all writers. An avid vinyl LP audiophile and science fiction connoisseur, he also loves to ski and allows golf to play him. Verde Mar now lives in the Sonoran Desert in Rancho Mirage, CA.

You can follow Verde Mar on social media platforms via @Tetrametracall1.


Verde Mar is a pseudonym